SCIENCE EXPLORER

ROCKS

SUPER COOL
SCIENCE
EXPERIMENTS:
ROCKS

by Sophie Lockwood

CHERRY LAKE PUBLISHING • ANN ARBOR, MICHIGAN

Published in the United States of America by
Cherry Lake Publishing
Ann Arbor, Michigan
www.cherrylakepublishing.com

Content Editor: Robert Wolffe, EdD,
Professor of Teacher Education,
Bradley University, Peoria, Illinois

Book design and illustration: The Design Lab

Photo Credits: Cover, ©Lightman/Dreamstime.com; page 4, ©H. Mark Weidman Photography/Alamy; page 7, ©iofoto, used under license from Shutterstock, Inc.; page 10, ©ARCTIC IMAGES/Alamy; page 11, ©Pancaketom/Dreamstime.com; page 15, ©Anson Hung, used under license from Shutterstock, Inc.; page 16, ©Index Stock/Alamy; page 20, ©Mg7/Dreamstime.com; page 24, ©Phil Degginger/Alamy

Library of Congress Cataloging-in-Publication Data
Lockwood, Sophie.
   Super cool science experiments : rocks / by Sophie Lockwood.
      p. cm.—(Science explorer)
   Includes index.
   ISBN-13: 978-1-60279-523-5   ISBN-10: 1-60279-523-1 (lib. bdg.)
   ISBN-13: 978-1-60279-601-0   ISBN-10: 1-60279-601-7 (pbk.)
 1. Rocks—Experiments—Juvenile literature.
2. Petrology—Juvenile literature. I. Title. II. Series.
QE432.2.L63 2009
   552.078—dc22   2009003321

Cherry Lake Publishing would like to acknowledge the work of The Partnership for 21st Century Skills. Please visit www.21stcenturyskills.org for more information.

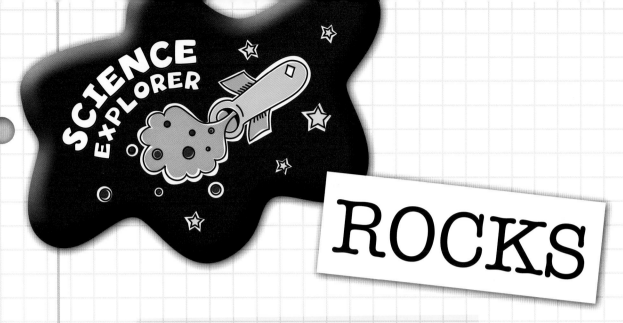

SCIENCE EXPLORER

ROCKS

TABLE OF CONTENTS

Long, Long Ago

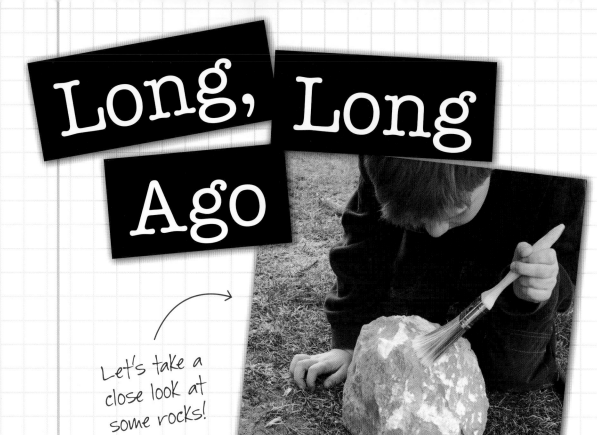

Let's take a close look at some rocks!

Rocks are gray or brown or black or speckled. They're hard. They hurt when you fall on them. They're also surprisingly interesting to study. How did they form? When did it happen? What are they made of? Scientists have experimented with rocks for centuries to find the answers to these questions.

If you've ever wondered about rocks and how they are made, you are also a scientist. Asking questions is step one in scientific exploration. In this book, you'll do experiments with rocks, model how they are formed, and find answers to some hard questions. You'll even learn how to design your own experiments!

First Things First

Good science depends on observations. Begin your experiments with what you already have seen and know. You already know more about rocks than you think. Maybe you know that some rocks formed millions of years ago. You have probably noticed that all rocks are not the same color. Some are solid colors, and some have several colors in them. Some rocks are jagged and sharp. Others are smooth to the touch.

When scientists design experiments, they must think very clearly. The way they think about problems is often called the scientific method. What is the scientific method? It's a step-by-step way of finding answers to specific questions. The steps don't always follow the same pattern.

Pick a rock, any rock.

5

Scientific method →

Sometimes scientists change their minds. The process often works something like this:

- **Step One:** A scientist gathers the facts and makes observations about one particular thing.
- **Step Two:** The scientist comes up with a question that is not answered by all the observations and facts.
- **Step Three:** The scientist creates a hypothesis. This is a statement of what the scientist thinks is probably the answer to the question.
- **Step Four:** The scientist tests the hypothesis. He or she designs an experiment to see whether the hypothesis is correct. The scientist does the experiment and writes down what happens.
- **Step Five:** The scientist draws a conclusion based on how the experiment turned out. The conclusion might be that the hypothesis is correct. Sometimes, though, the hypothesis is not correct. In that case, the scientist might develop a new hypothesis and another experiment.

In the following experiments, we'll see the scientific method in action. We'll gather some facts and observations about rocks. We'll develop a question and a hypothesis. Next, we'll come up with an experiment to see if our hypothesis is correct. We'll do the experiment. By the end of the experiment, we should know something new about rocks. Scientists, are you ready? Then rock on!

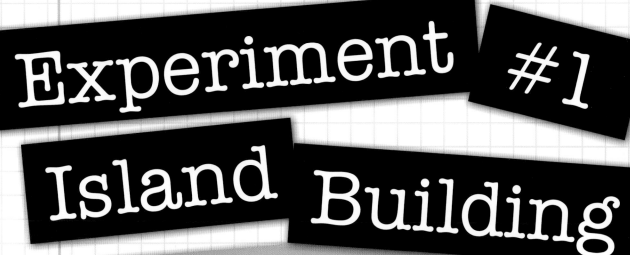

Experiment #1
Island Building

← Maui is just one of the islands that make up the state of Hawaii.

Have you ever wondered how islands pop up in the middle of the ocean? Look at the Hawaiian Islands on a map. They are too far away from North America to have broken off from the mainland. How did they get there?

Let's think about what we know. Several of the islands have active volcanoes. Volcanoes produce lava when they erupt. When lava cools, it becomes igneous rock. Igneous means "made from fire." Here's the question: Could lava pouring out of a volcano form an island? We can't actually perform an experiment with molten lava. But we can experiment to see if a hot, thick liquid can form a hard mass. We need a hypothesis. How about this one: **If we pour hot, thick sugar syrup into a bucket, it will harden into an "island."** Now we can set up an experiment to test the hypothesis.

Here's what you'll need:
- A bucket (a beach pail would work) filled with 4 inches (10 centimeters) of cold water
- 2 cups of sugar
- A large frying pan
- A wooden spoon
- An adult helper
- A pot holder

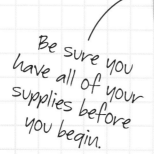

Be sure you have all of your supplies before you begin.

8

Have an adult help you with the hot pan!

Instructions:

1. Get the bucket of water ready, and set it in the kitchen sink.
2. Pour the sugar into a frying pan. Set the pan on the stove. You may want to have an adult help you.
3. Over medium-high heat, melt the sugar. Stir it with the wooden spoon. Don't stop stirring! How does the sugar change?
4. When the sugar is melted all the way and turned to liquid, take the pan over to the sink. Be sure to use a pot holder. Very slowly pour the liquid sugar syrup into the bucket of water. Watch what happens, and write down your observations.

Conclusion:

After you perform your experiment, you need to think about your results. A good scientist draws a conclusion about what happened. So think about it. What happened to the sugar syrup? Did you prove your hypothesis?

~ Surtsey is off the south coast of Iceland.

Islands can take thousands of years to form. Surtsey, an island off the coast of Iceland, formed very quickly, though. In May 1963, the undersea volcano Sutur began erupting. For months, the volcano spit lava, ash, cinders, and  into the northern Atlantic Ocean. On November 15, 1963, an island was born. The island of Surtsey rose from the ocean floor to the surface of the Atlantic in just 6 months. Today, Surtsey is a nature reserve, and scientists study how it continues to grow and change.

Experiment Making Rocks

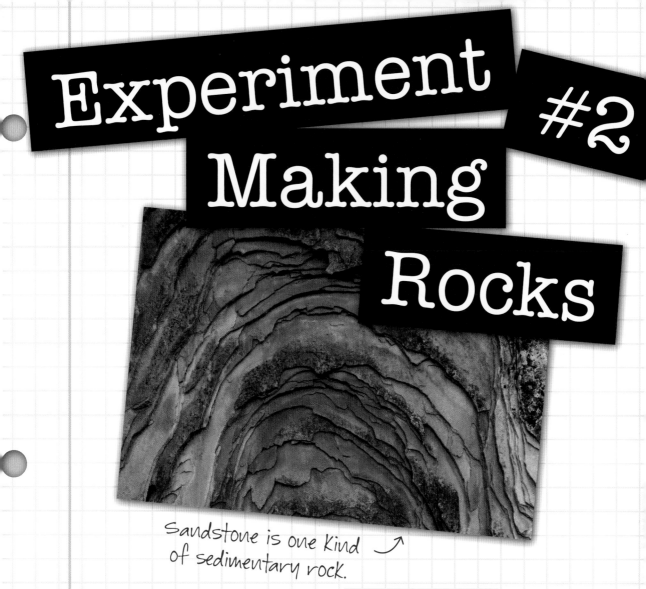

Sandstone is one kind of sedimentary rock. ↗

It took millions of years for sedimentary rocks to form on the floors of ancient seas. Sedimentary rocks often build in layers, called strata. The deepest layers in a large sedimentary rock formation are usually the oldest. Although we don't have a million years, we can make a model of sedimentary deposits. Here is your hypothesis: **No matter what materials sedimentary rocks are made of, the bottommost layers are the first to form.**

You can find kitty litter at a grocery store or pet store.

Here's what you'll need:

- 4 disposable drinking cups
- ½ cup of gravel or kitty litter
- 1¼ cups of plaster of Paris or dry spackle
- Water
- A wooden spoon
- The bottom half of a 2-liter soda bottle
- ¾ cups of sand
- Food coloring
- Scissors

Instructions:

1. You are about to compress millions of years of rock formation into about 15 minutes. In a disposable cup, mix together the gravel, ½ cup of plaster of Paris, and ¼ cup of water. Using the wooden spoon, stir it all together until it is mixed well.

2. Pour the mixture into the soda bottle. This is your first sedimentary deposit. It represents a deposit made up of rough rocks that have broken away from an area such as a rocky coastline.

3. In each of the other 3 disposable cups, mix ¼ cup of sand and ¼ cup of plaster of Paris. Add 5 drops of food coloring to each cup, making sure to use a different color for each cup. Add just enough water to wet the mixture. Stir the contents of each cup until they are mixed well.

Stir it up!

4. Pour the mixture from each cup into the soda bottle, one at a time. Write down the order of the colored mixtures as you pour them. These layers represent the buildup of finer particles and sediments.

5. Now, here's the hard part— let the soda bottle sit for 3 days. Do not move it or shake it.

6. Use scissors to cut the bottle away and look at the colors of the layers. You may want to have an adult help you with this part. Write down your observations.

Be careful not to disturb the layers when you cut away the bottle.

Conclusion:

Which layer is the oldest? Which layers are newest? Did you prove your hypothesis?

Sedimentary and igneous rock can also become metamorphic rock under the right conditions of heat and pressure. In nature, it is possible to have layers or sections of sedimentary, igneous, and metamorphic rock in the same area.

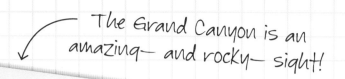
The Grand Canyon is an amazing— and rocky— sight!

The Grand Canyon was formed as a rushing river carved its way through deep layers of sedimentary rock. This happened over millions of years. The strata are different thicknesses and different colors. Each layer was deposited at a different time. Most of the rock you see at the Grand Canyon is sedimentary rock. But the Grand Canyon also has igneous and metamorphic rock. How old is the Grand Canyon? Scientists used to think it was about 6 million years old. In 2008, however, scientists from the University of New Mexico ran new experiments on eroded Grand Canyon rocks. They found that the Grand Canyon might be 16 million years old.

Experiment #3
Let's Twist

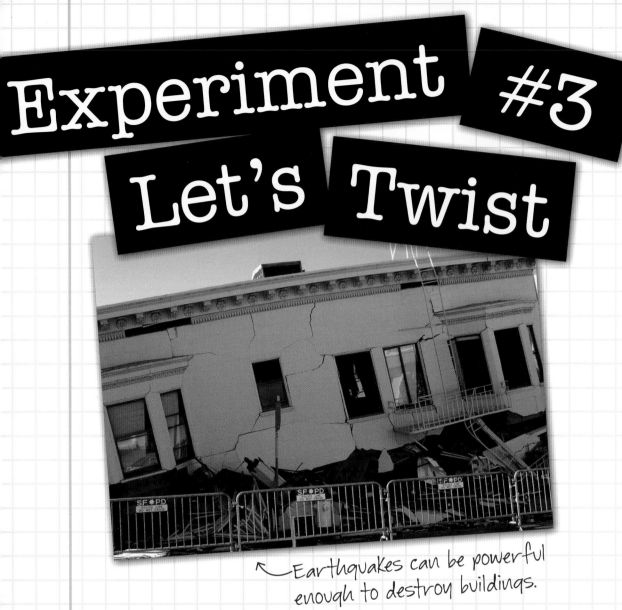

← Earthquakes can be powerful enough to destroy buildings.

You've proven that the bottom layer of sedimentary rock is the oldest. But suppose something happened to the rock? Earthquakes twist and turn rocks—cracking, breaking, and folding them. Could a major geological event such as an earthquake change the order of rock layers? Our hypothesis is this: **Major Earth events can change the shape and order of rock layers.**

Here's what you'll need:

- 3 different colors of modeling clay
- A piece of waxed paper or aluminum foil
- A rolling pin
- A marker
- A ruler
- A knife

Modeling clay can be found at a craft or art supply store.

Instructions:

1. Sometimes, an earthquake will push and press rock layers together. You are going to reproduce this event. Flatten one piece of modeling clay on the waxed paper. Roll it with the rolling pin until it is about ½ inch (1 cm) thick.
2. Put the next piece of clay on top of the flattened clay and roll it.
3. Put the last piece of clay on top of the first two and roll it.

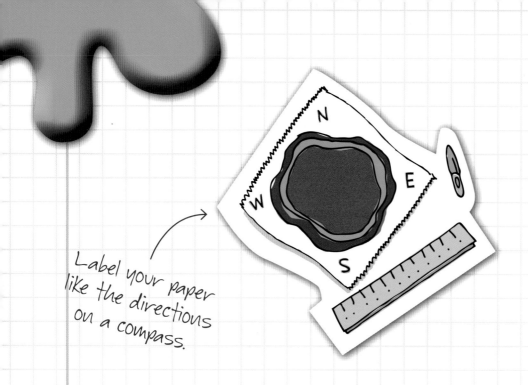

Label your paper like the directions on a compass.

4. Your three layers of clay are like layers of rock. On one edge of the waxed paper that is farthest away from you, use a marker to write "North." On the side closest to you, mark the paper "South." The right side is "East," and the left side is "West."

5. You are going to make a tiny earthquake. Hold the ruler by the middle. Place the long edge of the ruler along the edge of the clay nearest you. Hold the ruler at an angle so that the edge of the ruler touches the waxed paper. Use your other hand to hold the waxed paper down.

6. Slowly push the ruler along the waxed paper, underneath the clay layers. Scrape the clay from the edge nearest you toward the center, from South to North. Keep scraping with the ruler until you reach the North edge of the clay.

7. Using the knife, cut the clay once going North to South. Then cut the clay two or three times from East to West. Pull the pieces of clay apart where you cut them.

Conclusion:

Look at each piece of clay from all sides. What has changed? Write down your observations and draw a conclusion. You have just modeled what happens when a major event, such as an earthquake, changes Earth's rocky crust.

Try this experiment another way. After rolling the clay in layers, cut the clay in half. Fold one half over the other as if you were closing an open book. Cut again and look at the layers of rock. Is the bottom layer—the oldest—still on the bottom only? How have the layers changed?

Experiment #4

In the Days of Dinosaurs

↖ Fossils help us learn about dinosaurs and other living things from ancient times.

Scientists find many interesting things in the different layers of sedimentary rock. Fish, plants, insects, and even dinosaurs died in the muck that later became layers of sedimentary rock. The remains of these plants and animals formed fossils.

Most fossils formed at the bottom of ancient seas. That is why it is not surprising that most fossil remains are from shellfish. You can model fossil formations. Prove this hypothesis: **It is possible to form fossils of both shells and plants.**

Here's what you'll need:
- A shell
- A plant with small leaves, such as a fern or ivy
- Petroleum jelly
- A spoon
- 2 cups of plaster of Paris
- A small mixing bowl
- 2 small plastic cups

Get ready to make your own fossils!

Instructions:

1. Coat the back of the shell and one side of the plant with a thin layer of petroleum jelly.

2. Using a spoon, mix the plaster of Paris in a small mixing bowl according to directions. Pour half of the plaster mixture into each cup.

3. Press the shell halfway into the plaster in one cup. Make sure the side with the petroleum jelly is facing down.

4. In the other cup, press the plant halfway into the plaster. Again, be sure the side with the petroleum jelly is facing down.

5. Let the plaster set for one day.

6. Gently remove the shell and the fern. Which is easier to remove? Look at both fossils. Write down your observations.

Don't forget to record your observations.

Conclusion:

Did you prove your hypothesis? There are many different types of fossils. Fossils called imprints form when plants or animals push into soft mud or sand. It is as if they are stamping the surface. The shapes and details left behind may become preserved as the mud solidifies or becomes hard. This is different than when scientists discover fossilized bones or teeth. In a very simple way, you have made imprint fossils.

In 2006, scientists in Argentina found fossils of the neck bones, backbones, and tailbones from one of the largest known dinosaurs that ever lived. The dinosaur was a new species of *Titanosaur* (giant dinosaur). It was also a plant eater. One bone from the dinosaur's spine measures slightly more than 3.3 feet (1 meter) long. That's the height of an average four-year-old child. That's one big bone!

Experiment #5
Scratch It

↖ Some rocks are hard enough to scratch other rocks.

Suppose you were building a wall with some stones you found. Do you think it would help to know the hardness of these stones? Yes, some rocks are harder than others. Some rocks are so soft you can scratch them with your fingernail. Some have medium hardness and can be scratched with a pocketknife. Others are so hard that only a diamond will mark them. Hard stones are better for building because they last longer than soft ones.

Let's do an experiment to test the hardness of rocks. We'll use samples of chalk, limestone, and quartz. Which one do you think will be the hardest? Here are three possible hypotheses:

Hypothesis #1: Chalk is harder than limestone and quartz.

Hypothesis #2: Limestone is harder than chalk and quartz.

Hypothesis #3: Quartz is harder than chalk and limestone.

Here's what you'll need:
- Scissors
- Coarse sandpaper (60 grit will do)
- Pieces of chalk, limestone, and quartz
- A marker pen

Coarse sandpaper is best for this experiment. →

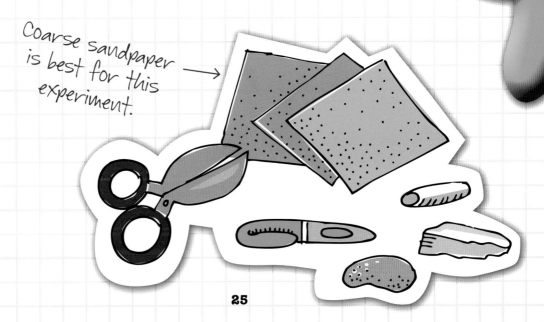

Instructions:

1. Use scissors to cut the sandpaper into squares that are about 3 inches (7.5 cm) on each side. You will need 3 squares, one for each rock sample.

2. Pick up your sample of chalk. Run your fingers over the surface to see how smooth or rough it is. Now use firm pressure and rub the chalk back and forth 20 times against the sandpaper. Use the marker to label that sandpaper square with the word "chalk."

3. Does the chalk crumble easily? Does the sandpaper leave scratches or other marks on it? Is the rock smoother after rubbing? Write down your observations.

4. Repeat steps 2 and 3 with the sample of limestone.

5. Repeat steps 2 and 3 with the sample of quartz.

Label each piece of sandpaper.

Conclusion:

Based on your observations, which rock was the hardest? Was your hypothesis correct? How do you know?

In 1812, German scientist Friedrich Mohs created a scale for testing the hardness of rocks and minerals. The Mohs scale is based on rocks that were commonly available to him at the time.

softest

Hardness	Example	Common form or use
1	Talc	Talcum powder
2	Gypsum	Plaster of Paris
3	Calcite	Limestone and most shells
4	Fluorite	Prevents tooth decay
5	Apatite	Used as a fertilizer
6	Orthoclase	Used in glasses and ceramics
7	Quartz	Semiprecious gems (tigereye, agate, amethyst, onyx, and others)
8	Topaz	Semiprecious gems
9	Corundum	Sapphires and rubies
10	Diamond	Used in jewelry and cutting tools

hardest

A rock can scratch any rock that has a lower hardness number.

Experiment #6

Do It Yourself!

You may come across rocks in your backyard, in a nearby playground, or when you travel. Keep a kit handy for experimenting on them. All you need for this kit is a piece of coarse-grit sandpaper, a plastic bottle of vinegar, and a small magnifying glass. As with all experiments, be careful when experimenting with rocks. Make sure you do not get vinegar in your eyes, for example.

Always keep an eye out for interesting rocks.

When you find a rock, test for hardness with the sandpaper. Is the rock hard or soft? Find out if the rock has calcium carbonate (lime) in it by putting a few drops of vinegar on it. If there is lime present, the vinegar will bubble. Is lime present? Look at the rock through the magnifying glass. Is the color even, or are there different bits of color in the rock?

When you find an unusual rock, test it using the scientific method. It's easy, it's fun, and you'll surprise your parents and friends with what you know. You can show them that science is all around you—even in rocks.

If the vinegar bubbles, the rock has lime in it.

GLOSSARY

conclusion (kuhn-KLOO-zhuhn) a final decision, thought, or opinion

hypothesis (hy-POTH-uh-sihss) a logical guess about what will happen in an experiment

igneous rock (IG-nee-uhss ROK) rock produced when hot lava cools down and becomes hard

metamorphic rock (met-uh-MAWR-fik ROK) rock, such as marble, that has been changed by intense heat or pressure

method (METH-uhd) a way of doing something

observations (ob-zur-VAY-shuhnz) things that are seen or noticed with one's senses

pumice (PUHM-iss) a light-colored, porous volcanic rock

sedimentary rocks (sed-uh-MEN-tuh-ree ROKS) rocks, such as sandstone or siltstone, resulting from the deposit of soil or rock particles

FOR MORE INFORMATION

BOOKS

Driscoll, Michael, and Dennis Driscoll. *A Child's Introduction to the Environment: The Air, Earth, and Sea Around Us—Plus Experiments, Projects, and Activities You Can Do to Help Our Planet!* New York: Black Dog & Leventhal Publishers, 2008.

VanCleave, Janice. *Janice VanCleave's Super Science Challenges: Hands-On Inquiry Projects for Schools, Science Fairs, or Just Plain Fun!* San Francisco: Jossey-Bass, 2008.

Williams, Zella. *Experiments on Rocks and the Rock Cycle.* New York: PowerKids Press, 2007.

WEB SITES

Crystal Clear Science Fair Projects

www.crystal-clear-science-fair-projects.com/science-projects-for-kids.html

Look for other science projects that deal with rocks, soil, or geology at this fun Web site

Rocks for Kids: Info & Photos

www.rocksforkids.com/RFK/Rocks&Minerals.html

For photos and information about many different rocks and minerals

INDEX

About the → Author

In addition to writing books, Sophie Lockwood does experiments in her kitchen all the time! Although most of the experiments are called dinner, Sophie and her granddaughter actually did every experiment in this book. Sophie lives in South Carolina with her husband and enjoys reading, playing bridge, and watching movies when she isn't writing.